Cook Up a RAD future

You ar amazing and I can't wait to see what you do with your life :)
Happy birthday
♡Barbara

REVOLUTION RAD GIRL

WRITTEN BY:

Sharita Manickam

PHOTO ILLUSTRATIONS BY:

Jennifer Elliott Bruno

To Leela and Ella - May you always rise above doubt and go after your dreams! - S.M.

To Henry - Never doubt the value of being yourself and the power of encouraging others to do the same. - J.E.B.

ISBN 978-0-692-19018-0 (hardcover)

Cover Photo Illustrations by Jennifer Elliott Bruno
Jacket Photo of Sharita Manickam by Jennifer Elliott Bruno
Jacket Photo of Jennifer Elliott Bruno by Rena McCaslin
Endsheet Design by Jane Marsilio

Printed in China

RAD Girl Revolution, LLC

For more information, visit www.radgirlrevolution.com

There's a RAD GIRL REVOLUTION thanks to those who raised their voices.

They paved the way for girls today to grow up having choices.

Once you find your passion, you can follow your own path.

Your career can be in business, or in science, art, or math!

So set your mind and focus on the dreams you will pursue,

And you will be unstoppable, there's nothing you can't do!

You can be an acrobat,
and swing on a trapeze,
Or balance on the tightrope
with amazing skill and ease.

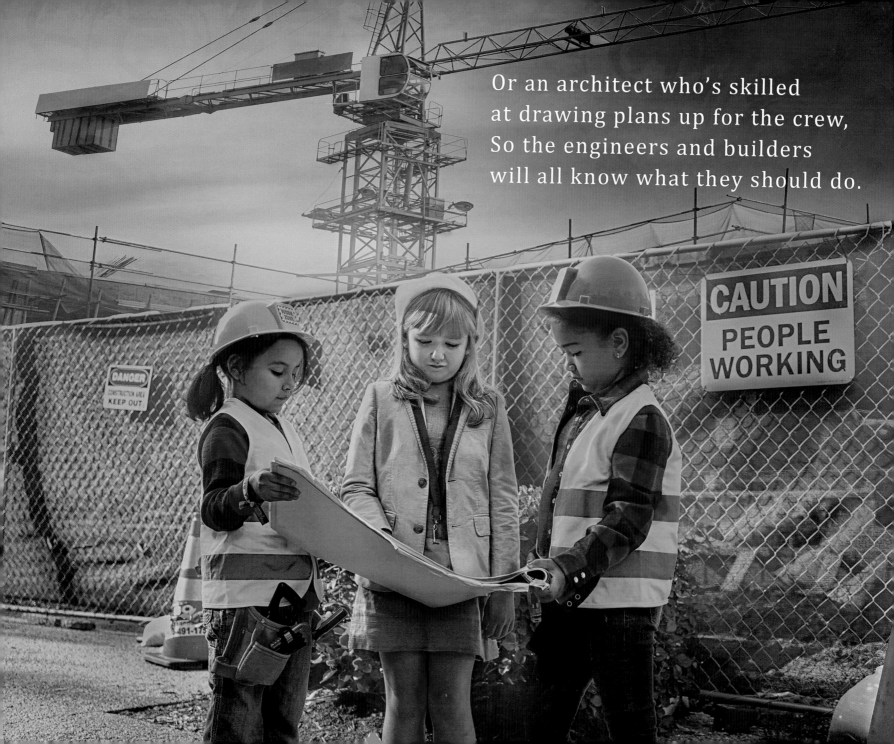

Or an architect who's skilled
at drawing plans up for the crew,
So the engineers and builders
will all know what they should do.

Or what about an artist
with your very own technique,
Creating a true masterpiece
that's timeless and unique?

As an astronaut in space,
you'll get to float among the stars,
And land upon the Moon
or be the first to walk on Mars!

You can be on Broadway, starring in the latest play,
Getting lots of praise and rave reviews every single day.

Rise Above Doubt ✓
Reach Any Dream ✓

#girlbosstour

An ambitious CEO, so successful, smart, and able,
Surrounded by the sharpest business minds around the table.

An award-winning chef,
with entrées meant to savor,
And delicious desserts
that are bursting full of flavor.

Or what about a dentist,
helping teeth stay strong and bright,
Telling patients they should brush them
in the morning and at night?

A clever, bright detective,
finding each and every clue,
And piecing them together
to uncover what is true.

A Hollywood director, shouting "QUIET ON THE SET!" And working with your crew to make the greatest movie yet!

A kind and caring doctor,
helping patients mend and heal,
By listening and curing
any pain that they may feel.

A dedicated farmer,
plowing hayfields, seeding oats,
You can harvest fields of corn,
milk the cows, and feed the goats.

What about a firefighter,
battling smoke and blazes?
Saving people, dogs, and cats-
oh, your bravery amazes!

An inventor with ideas
for new gadgets that are great,
You'll be changing the whole world
with all the things you will create.

Or how about a judge who makes decisions that are fair,
By ruling on your cases with attention, sense, and care?

You can be a lawyer,
and defend with all your might.
When it's something you believe in,
it is always worth the fight.

Or a magnificent magician, entertaining with such flair,
As your assistant is levitated high up in the air!

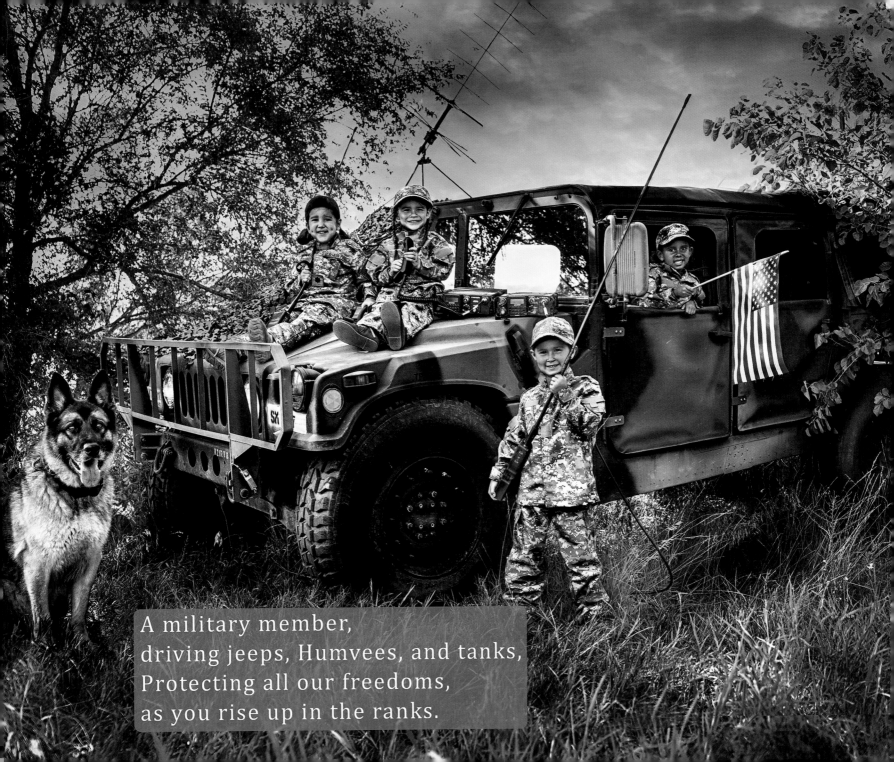

A military member,
driving jeeps, Humvees, and tanks,
Protecting all our freedoms,
as you rise up in the ranks.

A musician in a band,
you will be basking in the fame,
While performing on a stage,
as all your fans call out your name.

A young Olympic athlete,
staying focused, strong, and bold.
Your training and your confidence
will help you win the gold.

Or a paleontologist, who digs in dirt and sand,
Finding fossils of old dinosaurs that used to roam this land.

As the pilot of an airplane, you'll be soaring to new heights,
Flying passengers on trips while you are taking in the sights!

An officer who's sworn to always serve and to protect,
You'll help the whole community while earning much respect.

Or the President who's signing a new law into place,
Giving equal rights to *all*, no matter gender, age, or race.

A professor in a great big hall, with lectures you prepare,
Your work expands young minds with all the knowledge that you share.

You can be a gifted programmer, who codes all types of apps,
Developing fun games and even interactive maps.

A reporter at your desk, or giving updates from the scene,
Delivering the news to every television screen.

BREAKING NEWS

"That's one small step for man,
one giant leap for mankind."

WOMEN
WALK
ON THE
MOON

RAD GIRL
REVOLUTION NEWS

52 0.09% ... MADAM PRESIDENT AWARDS RAD GIRL ASTRONAUTS AT WHITE HO

You can be a brilliant scientist, who's looking for an answer. Your research and experiments could find a cure for cancer.

A banker working Wall Street,
giving clients great advice,
And helping with investments
so they'll get the fairest price.

A best-selling author, signing books for your young readers,
Hoping you inspire a generation of RAD leaders!

The RAD GIRL REVOLUTION is now full steam ahead.

It's time to tell the world and let the message spread!

Say it LOUD! Say it *proud*!

SCREAM IT!

YELL IT!

SHOUT!

"I'M A RAD GIRL!

I WILL RISE ABOVE DOUBT!"

SHOUT it from the rooftops!

Let us hear you SCREAM!

"I'M A RAD GIRL!

I CAN REACH ANY DREAM!"

Acknowledgments

TO OUR RAD GIRL MODELS: Thank you for being YOU! You were incredible! Each and every one of you have inspired us beyond measure! Wherever life takes you, never forget that you are a *RAD GIRL*!

. . . AND TO OUR FIVE RAD BOY MODELS: We didn't forget you! Keep being the amazing RAD boys that you are and continue to support the RAD girls in your life!

ACROBAT: **Ruby**   ARCHITECT: **Stella** (architect) **Emma and Gabrielle** (engineers/builders)   ARTIST: **Francesca**   ASTRONAUT: **Teagan and Olivia**   BROADWAY STAR: **Izabella**   CEO: **Harper** (CEO) **Emma, Sonya, Madison, Brianna, Elliotte, and Maria** (executives)   CHEF: **Sofia**   DENTIST: **Ruby** (dentist) **Anna Rose** (hygienist) **Abigail** (patient)   DETECTIVE: **Olivia and Sofia**   DIRECTOR: **Amit** (script supervisor) **Emma** (camera operator**)** **Juliette** (director) **Leela** (clapper loader)   DOCTOR: **Lydia** (doctor) **Valentina** (patient)   FARMER: **Sterling**   FIREFIGHTER: **Luna**   INVENTOR: **Layla**   JUDGE: **Lola**   LAWYER: **Lucy and Emma** (lawyers) **Lola** (judge)   MAGICIAN: **Lily** (magician) **Eve** (assistant)   MILITARY MEMBER: **Akemi, Victoria, Emma, and Teagan**   MUSICIAN: **Roya** (drummer) **Josephine** (singer) **Elana** (keyboardist) **Annalisa** (guitarist)   OLYMPIAN: **Zoey and Charlotte** (boxers) **Ava** (referee)   PALEONTOLOGIST: **Sabrina and Hayley**   PILOT: **Amelia and Mariana**   POLICE OFFICER: **Juliet**   PRESIDENT: **Leela** (President) **Alexandra, Imogen, Nely, Juliet, Gwenhwyfar, and Madeline** (president's cabinet)   PROFESSOR: **Ciara** (professor) **Valentina, Leela, Fitzgerald, Truman, AJ, Benjamin, Lydia, Clara, Henry, and Luke** (students)   PROGRAMMER: **Asha**   REPORTER: **Liliana and Mila** (news anchors) **Teagan and Olivia** (astronauts)   SCIENTIST: **Sadie**   WALL STREET BANKER: **Tabitha**   WRITER: **Sophie** (author) **Harper, Asha, and Annalisa** (readers)

We would like to thank the following people and establishments for opening their doors to us for our photo shoots:

• **Automatic Studios** • **Chelsea Pediatric Dentistry** • **Children's Museum of Manhattan** • **Courtroom of Hon. Melissa C. Jackson** • **Cradle of Aviation Museum** • **The DeHaven Family Farm** • **Engine Co. 305, Hook & Ladder Co. 151** • **Kew & Willow Books** • **Little Pulp: Printmaking Workshop for Kids** • **Long Island Children's Museum** • **McConnell Air Force Base** • **NYIT College of Osteopathic Medicine** • **The Starkin Family** • **TITLE Boxing Club of Forest Hills** • **Tuscan Hills**

A million thanks to the **parents of our models** and our 650 and counting **Kickstarter** and **Indiegogo InDemand backers** for supporting this project! We couldn't have done this without you! And a huge shout out to our local community of **Forest Hills, Queens**! We are so grateful for all the support we have received from friends new and old! We ♥ you!

RAD GIRL REVOLUTIONARIES

These *RAD GIRLS* are **R**esilient **A**mbitious **D**reamers. They will **R**ise **A**bove **D**oubt and can **R**each **Any D**ream!
We believe in the limitless potential of *all* the *RAD GIRLS* in the world. We believe in YOU!

Aleena Smith	Cece Estess	Genevieve Elizabeth Metzger	Molly Rose
Alia Rose Abdullah	Charley Jude Wilmoth	Haley Henningson	Na'ilah Yvonne Furqan
Alice Holeman	Charlotte & Sawyer Rose	Harper Cuva	Nolyn Corkey
Allie Martell	Charlotte Nichols	Hayley Huffman	Obaasan Dawn
Alyssa Yunis	Christina Grace Acosta Ware	Hazel Jane Altwies	Parker Riley Sachs
Amaya Resham Abdullah	Daisy Hampton	Ivy Fujibayashi	Reagan Bruno
Ami Varghese	Dorothy Holeman	Izabella & Valentina Sampietro	Riley Magyar
Annabelle & Aria Eccleston	Dr. Sadhana Chheda	Jovie James Neeley	River Moon Quinn
Annabelle Jane Hebert	Eden Gaetano	Julliette Martell	Rosalie June Coniglio
Ashley Arancibia	Elena Renee Lozano	Kennedy DeVito	Rosalina A. Castro
Aubrey Eure	Ella Olivia Moore	Kiana Ma	Sabrina A. Hobson
Audrey Grace Attanasio	Elliotte M. Clark	Lauren Smith	Sadie Long
Ava Grace Rivera	Emily Moreno	Leela Mia Moore	Samara Martell
Ava M. Steinau	Emma Jacqueline Holle	Leilani Rey	Sarah Fischthal
Ava Rose Lyon	Essie Funk	Lila Tuv	Soliel Abella Escamilla
Brooke Bushner	Eva Clara Valentin	Liliana, Emi, and Mai DeGrottole	Sophie & Sadie Cohen
Brooklyn Murawski	Eva Jade Campbell	Lilly Martell	Stephanie Chambers
Callie Elspeth Priddy	Evelyn Daniel	Lorelei Virginia Kay Foreman	Stephanie R. Eggers
Carissa Gorelick	Evelyn V. Engel	Lucienne Castillo	Sydney Seeger
Caroline Glismann	Everly Lynn Draina	Lucy Isenberg	Taylor E. Steinau
Catriona Nolan	Fiona Elaine Poiry	Luisa-Elizabeth Marianna Paulson	Tita Reiko
Caylee Gorelick	Frankie Farnsworth	Mia Imani Watts	Zoey Martell